Little Waves

Haiku and Senryu

by Andrew Terrell

ISBN: 978-93-6354-025-5

First Edition: 2024
Rs. 200/-

Cyberwit.net
HIG 45 Kaushambi Kunj, Kalindipuram
Allahabad - 211011 (U.P.) India
http://www.cyberwit.net
Tel: +(91) 9415091004
E-mail: info@cyberwit.net

Printed at Repro India Limited.

Dedicated to Christina P. T. Nguyễn

1. Skagit County and Whatcom County

dead butterfly
kids walking back
from summer camp

field of tall grass
dirt flies up from a hole
where the dog must be

stepping out from car
slipping on ice—
restaurant closed

men arguing
by a shopping center
lurching intersection

stiff back
sound of a drawer
sliding smooth

garage door opens
cleaning rat poop
in a winter jacket

outside the window
snow on the pines
a squirrel jumps

talking laps
about finances
village cemetery

gray river
yielding on the phone
to a banker

roof leak
on wood stove
cat stretches

landscaping
for martial arts teacher
chasing the lawnmower

winter grass
around the van
pile of tools

a plume of smoke
from the fireplace
jealous of my friends

summer chatter
no one but my wife
in my tai chi class

wistful story
reaching for the knob
to turn up her volume

thinking on porch
after spring storm
sporadic drip tap

sunset and thunder
behind the server
a smile

boots under table
trying to avoid
the news

stalling truck
a young buck hobbles
through autumn leaves

cold morning
king salmon ripping
up a waterfall

2. Hawai‘i

little waves
bottom up to shore
the old turtle

did I insult her?
rain playing loudly
with the mud

counting desperately
haiku in a notebook
the rain comes back

small moon
covered by a patch of clouds
packing bags again

cloud break
a spider drops a line
to repair its web

thwack
a tropical leaf
begins to drip water

walking past pigeons
spinning and flying
the pizza crust

dangling potato bug
spider watching
the lazy breeze

grasses bend
perfect in the sunlight
quitting poetry

headlamp–
a sudden confrontation
with a moth's orange eye

four snorkelers
below a cliff
wind sweeps the Pacific

peacock bellows
retreating inside
–edge of the world

a bird's single leap
today the land is full
of hot air

woman in window
sneaking at night
to pick a grapefruit

the dog lowers its leg
continues trotting
pink flowers

black bull stands
in front of his herd
–screaming from the field

bus bladder
watching the pigeon carry
what's too big

clearing the mulch pile
ants swarming
a brown beetle

all morning watching
blue sky to the left
storm clouds to the right

last of the hay
carried to the truck
golden full moon

3. Dharug Country

new neighborhood
red sunrise
the fleeing cockatoo

lorikeet screaming
through the morning
too bitter to speak

still afternoon
sound of a pelican
scratching its head

approaching storm
hurrying across the yard
three magpies

unboxing
new air purifier
packing fumes

same old argument
floating through my head
trash bag in the wind

a bored dog
a caught lizard
midday heat

labor, day three
back in the saddle
of bedside chair

half past midnight
pouring tea
into a full mug

magpies speaking
softly in the dark
nursing baby

laying through dawn
until my bones ache
breath of my child

mushrooms
growing on television–
who goes to bed first?

nervous starling
at edge of bath
my old stories

shaving anger
the steady rhythm
of currawong wings

morning commuters
a sweet mango pit
clatters to the floor

friends walking in silence
smooth stones
in the riverbed

slow, gray afternoon
telling to the window
stories of my neighbors

quiet town
the pop of a baby
sucking her thumb

returning home
wind flaps
a loose rose petal

voices of children
a white tail
wagging through the door

The following wonderful journals originally published these poems:

bus bladder...	Asahi Haikuist Network, June 2, 2023
small moon...	Asahi Haikuist Network, June 16, 2023
lorikeet screaming...	Asahi Haikuist Network, December 15, 2023
little waves...	Autumn Moon Haiku Journal, Volume 6:2
last of the hay...	cattails, October 2023
approaching storm...	Cold Moon Journal, November 23, 2023
cloud break...	Enchanted Garden Haiku Journal, Issue 2
garage door opens...	Failed Haiku, Issue 73
did I insult her?...	Failed Haiku, Issue 91
same old argument...	Failed Haiku, Issue 93
unboxing...	Failed Haiku, Issue 94
clearing the mulch pile...	Modern Haiku, 54.2
still afternoon...	Modern Haiku, 55.1
all morning watching...	NeverEnding Story, October 12, 2023
field of tall grass...	Presence, Issue 72

dead butterfly...	Presence, Issue 75
new neighborhood...	seashores, Issue 11
stepping out from car...	Taj Mahal Review, Volume 24:2
men arguing...	Taj Mahal Review, Volume 24:2
stiff back...	Taj Mahal Review, Volume 24:2
talking laps...	Taj Mahal Review, Volume 24:2
gray river...	Taj Mahal Review, Volume 24:2
roof leak...	Taj Mahal Review, Volume 24:2
landscaping...	Taj Mahal Review, Volume 24:2
winter grass...	Taj Mahal Review, Volume 24:2
counting desperately...	tsuri-dōrō, Issue 16
thwack...	Under the Bashō, April 11, 2023
walking past pigeons...	Under the Bashō, April 11, 2023

www.ingramcontent.com/pod-product-compliance
Ingram Content Group UK Ltd.
Pitfield, Milton Keynes, MK11 3LW, UK
UKHW041316190726
13845UKWH00025B/302

9 789363 540255